THIS IS
Kaua'i

THIS IS
Kaua'i
Visions of the Islands

THIS IS
Kaua'i

Visions of the Islands

• • • • • • • • •

Photography by
Douglas Peebles

Mutual Publishing

Note: In the past, written Hawaiian language did not use macrons and glottal stops. The practice is generally accepted today as an aid to proper pronunciation and spelling. Diacritical markings as found in *Place Names of Hawaii* and in Pukui and Elbert's *Hawaiian Dictionary* have been added where appropriate.

Library of Congress Catalog Card
Number: 2003100929

ISBN 1-56647-594-5

First Printing, May 2003
Second Printing, October 2004
2 3 4 5 6 7 8 9

All photos © by Douglas Peebles
Design by Jane Hopkins

Mutual Publishing, LLC
1215 Center Street, Suite 210
Honolulu, Hawaii 96816
Ph: (808) 732-1709
Fax: (808) 734-4094
e-mail: mutual@mutualpublishing.com
www.mutualpublishing.com

Printed in Korea

Introduction

Mist shimmers in the lehua forests, and sweeps through canyons and valleys lush with emerald light. In the distance, across myriad folds in the high mountains, waterfalls drop straight from the clouds. These are the treasured images of Kaua'i, the Garden Island, a place of wild surf, breathtaking iron-oxide cliffs, and green hills cut by Hawai'i's only true rivers.

Located 100 miles north of O'ahu, it is the oldest of the island chain, and therefore the most sculpted and vegetated. Kaua'i ka moku kahiko, the saying goes, Kaua'i the ancient land.

Because of its remoteness and penchant for storms and rainfall, the island has retained much of what old Hawai'i used to be: sleepy towns, open markets, few tourists. On Kaua'i there are layers of cultures that date back millennia, starting with a lost race that predated the Hawaiians. The only evidence we have of these people is the stone ruins they left behind on these shores. Here too is the spot at Waimea where Captain James Cook, in 1778, made his startling discovery of the Sand-

▼▲▼▲▼▲▼▲▼▲▼▲▼▲▼▲▼▲▼▲▼▲▼▲▼▲▼▲▼

wich Islands, and met the northernmost chiefs of a thriving Polynesian kingdom. Near Cook's anchorage lies a dilapidated Russian fort that symbolizes the range of foreigners who have made Kaua'i their home.

What they found here—and what still exists beyond the sugar mills, shopping centers, and modern resorts—is the enduring splendor of the land itself.

No one has chanted and written about Kaua'i more eloquently than the Hawaiians. In their wisdom and words the landscape becomes poetry.

This is Kaua'i blends the proverbs and exhortations of the Hawaiian people with the photographic talent of Douglas Peebles in a presentation keepsake, a photo album of images and words to entreat the senses and stimulate memories.

E komo mai a Kaua'i nei, welcome to beloved Kaua'i. May you witness its *noe lehua* (the misty lehua rain), the narrows of Waimea Canyon, and the cloud-filled hanging valleys of Mount Wai'ale'ale.

Kalalau Trail

Beautiful is Kaua'i beyond compare,
She sends forth a bud in the summit of Wai'ale'ale,
She flowered in the heights of Kawaikini,
Her strength radiates in awful splendor from the Alaka'i;
Though I weary, though I faint, she renews my
strength in her soft petals.

chant honoring Wai'ale'ale

—Edward Joesting
Kauai: The Separate Kingdom

FROM THE Sky

· · · · · · ·

Kapa'a

He pūko'a ku no ka moana.

A large rock standing in the sea.

(Said of a person who is unchangeable and very determined.)

—Hawaiian Proverb, *'Ōlelo No'eau Hawaiian
Proverbs & Poetical Sayings*

Moku'ae'ae Island

Kalalau Beach

He mā‘ona moku.

A satisfaction with the land.

*(Said of a person contented with what he has,
as a chief is satisfied with his domain.)*

—Hawaiian Proverb, *ʻŌlelo Noʻeau Hawaiian
Proverbs & Poetical Saying*

Lā wa'i Valley

Līhu'e

E kuahui like i ka hana.

Let everybody pitch in and
work together.

—Hawaiian Proverb,
*'Ōlelo No'eau Hawaiian
Proverbs & Poetical Sayings*

Ni'ihau

Niʻihau i ke kīkū.

Niʻihau leans back firmly.

(Niʻihau people are independent.)

—Hawaiian Proverb,
ʻŌlelo Noʻeau Hawaiian Proverbs & Poetical Sayings

25

Lehua Island

Kalalau Valley

FLOWING
Water
. . . .

Ka wai hālau o Wailua.

The expansive waters of
Wailua.

*(Wailua, Kauaʻi, is the land of
large streams.)*

—Hawaiian Proverb,
*ʻŌlelo Noʻeau Hawaiian
Proverbs & Poetical Sayings*

Wailua River

Hanamāʻulu Beach Park

Kalalau Stream

He pūnāwai kahe wale
ke aloha.

Love is a spring that
flows freely.

*(Love is without bounds
and exists for all.)*

—Hawaiian Proverb,
*'Ōlelo No'eau Hawaiian
Proverbs & Poetical Sayings*

Kūlele ke ʻehu kai i ka makani.

The sprays are a-flying in the wind.

(What wrath!)

—Hawaiian Proverb, *ʻŌlelo Noʻeau Hawaiian Proverbs & Poetical Sayings*

Spouting Horn

VERDANT
Lands

· · · · · · ·

'Ōhi'a Forest

Hanalei Valley

Hanalei has been
likened by some to Paradise,
and by others to the Vale of
Kaschmir [sic]. Everyone who
sees it raves about it. "See
Hanalei and die," is the feeling
of the islanders, and certainly I
was not disappointed, nor
should I be with Paradise
itself were it even a
shade less fair!

—Isabella L. Bird
Six Months in the Sandwich Islands

Hā'upu mauna
kilohana i ka la'i.

Hā'upu, a mountain
outstanding in the calm.

*(Said of a person of outstanding
achievement. Also used in praise of
Hā'upu, Kaua'i.)*

—Hawaiian Proverb,
*'Ōlelo No'eau Hawaiian
Proverbs & Poetical Sayings*

Hāʻupu Mountain Range

The Hawaiians were sensitive to the world around them,
to the hills, the streams, the trees, the seashore, the clouds.
They chanted of these things, asking for protection, using them
as symbols, or simply celebrating their beauty.

—Edward Joesting
Kauai: The Separate Kingdom

Olokele Canyon

Wailua Falls

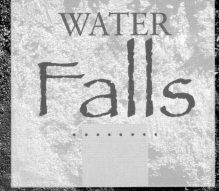

WATER
Falls
· · · · · · · ·

Kawaikini

Hoʻomoe wai
kāhi ke kāoʻo.

Let all travel
together like water
flowing in one
direction.

—Hawaiian Proverb,
*ʻŌlelo Noʻeau Hawaiian
Proverbs & Poetical Sayings*

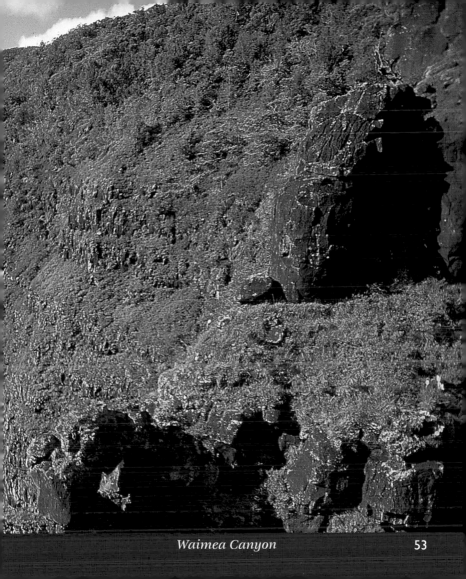

Waimea Canyon

There is a rough plateau atop the island of Kaua'i
and there is no other place like it in the world. Rising almost
from the very center of the island, this mountain peak is 5,148
feet tall. At the top is a solitary, windy, rain-ravaged plateau.
There is no doubt the mountain with its unique
plateau of gullies and knolls dominates the island of Kaua'i.
The mountain takes its name from a pond on the peak,
Wai'ale'ale, a Rippling on the Water.

—Edward Joesting
Kauai: The Separate Kingdom

Mt. Wai'ale'ale

'Ōpaeka'a Falls

Kalalau Valley

RISING

Peaks

· · · · · · · ·

Nāpali Coast

Mt. Wai'ale'ale

Ka ua Noelehua o Waiʻaleʻale.

The Misty-*lehua* rain of Waiʻaleʻale.

(The rain of Waiʻaleʻale that moistens the lehua *blossoms there.)*

—Hawaiian Proverb, *ʻŌlelo Noʻeau Hawaiian Proverbs*
& Poetical Sayings

Alaka'i Wilderness

Kauai, from the sea, is green and rose,
the bright volcanic earth showing through the rich
vegetation which has caused its inhabitants to claim for it the
name given to an unidentified island somewhere in these seas
by an early Spanish navigator: the Garden Island.

—Clifford Gessler
"Kauai and the 'Wettest Spot'" from *Hawaii: Isles of Enchantment*

Nāpali Coast

We turned up
between red-banked ditches
in which water apparently
flowed uphill, to look down
from a rocky point into the
tremendous chasm of Waimea.
Great conical ridges stood like
pillars, their sides tinted in
blending or contrasting or
delicately shaded hues; the
winding distances were misty
lavender; a bright ribbon of
stream coiled half a mile below.
Shadows of clouds painted light
and dark the various reds and
yellows of the cliffs. For
twenty-five miles that canyon
stretched before us, a vast hall
sculptured by the gods.

—Clifford Gessler
"Kauai and the 'Wettest Spot'"
from *The Spell of Hawaii*

Waimea Canyon

Nounou (Sleeping Giant)

Pūkoʻa kani ʻāina.

A hard rock of the land.

(Said of a strong fighter who destroys others but is himself impossible to destroy.)

Hawaiian Proverb,
*ʻŌlelo Noʻeau Hawaiian
Proverbs & Poetical Sayings*

Nāpali Coast

A DAY AT THE
Beach

· · · · · · · ·

Wailua Beach

Kalalau Beach

He ʻehu wāwae no
kalani.

A trace of the
heavenly one's
footsteps.

*(The rain, the rainbow,
and other signs seen
when a chief is abroad
are tokens of his
recognition by the
gods.)*

—Hawaiian Proverb,
*ʻŌlelo Noʻeau Hawaiian
Proverbs & Poetical Sayings*

Hā'ena Beach

Maika'i Kaua'i,
hemolele i ka
mālie.

Beautiful Kaua'i,
peaceful in the
calm.

(Line from a chant.)

—Hawaiian Proverb,
*'Ōlelo No'eau Hawaiian
Proverbs & Poetical Sayings*

'Anini Beach

I hoʻokāhi ka umauma, hoʻokāhi ke aloha.

All abreast together, one in love.

(All united in harmony and love.)

—Hawaiian Proverb, *ʻŌlelo Noʻeau Hawaiian*
Proverbs & Poetical Sayings

Nāpali Beach

Kalalau Beach

Nāwiliwili

Poho pono nā pe'a heke a ku ana.

A well-filled topsail helped him to arrive.

(Said of a fast traveler.)

—Hawaiian Proverb, *'Ōlelo No'eau Hawaiian Proverbs & Poetical Sayings*

Kalalau Beach

Kē'ē Beach

Aia nō i ke kō a ke au.

Whichever way the current
goes.

(Time will tell.)

—Hawaiian Proverb,
*'Ōlelo No'eau Hawaiian
Proverbs & Poetical Sayings*

Pāpa'a Bay

Hanalei taro fields

ONLY ON
Kaua'i

. . . .

Ka ipu o ka 'ike.

The gourd of wisdom.

(A wise man.)

—Henry P. Judd
Hawaiian Proverbs and Riddles

Ipu

Fisherman at Po'ipu

He iʻa kokoke kā
ka lawaiʻa.

A fisherman always
finds fish nearby.

*(Said of one who can
get what he wants
because he is smart.)*

—Hawaiian Proverb,
*ʻŌlelo Noʻeau Hawaiian
Proverbs & Poetical Sayings*

97

Tree tunnel lining Maluhia Road to Poʻipū

'Oni kalalea ke ku a
ka lāʻau loa.

The tall tree stands above
the others.

*(Said of a person of outstanding
achievements.)*

—Hawaiian Proverb,
*ʻŌlelo Noʻeau Hawaiian
Proverbs & Poetical Sayings*

Hanalei plantation home

Dolphins

Pi'i ka ihu o ka nai'a i ka makani.

The nose of the dolphin rises toward the wind.

(Said of one who is haughty.)

—Hawaiian Proverb, 'Ōlelo No'eau Hawaiian
Proverbs & Poetical Sayings

Ua lehulehu a manomano ka 'ikena a ka Hawai'i.

Great and numerous is the knowledge of the Hawaiians.

—Hawaiian Proverb,
'Ōlelo No'eau Hawaiian Proverbs & Poetical Sayings

Wailua State Park Heiau

Smith's Tropical Paradise

Ka pouhana.

The main post.

*(The person on whom others
depend for leadership, guidance, and help—
the mainstay of the family or group.)*

—Hawaiian Proverb,
'Ōlelo No'eau Hawaiian Proverbs & Poetical Sayings

Kīlauea Lighthouse

Hanapēpē salt ponds

Bibliography

Bird, Isabella L. *Six Months in the Sandwich Islands*. Honolulu: Mutual Publishing, 1998.

Gessler, Clifford. "Kauai and the 'Wettest Spot'" in A. Grove Day and Carl Stroven, eds. *The Spell of Hawaii*. New York: Meredith Press, 1968.

Joesting, Edward. Kauai: The Separate Kingdom. Honolulu: University of Hawai'i Press, 1984.

Judd, Henry P. *Hawaiian Proverbs and Riddles*. Honolulu: Bernice P. Bishop Museum, Bulletin 77, 1930.

Pukui, Mary Kawena. *'Ōlelo No'eau: Hawaiian Proverbs & Poetical Sayings*. Honolulu: Bishop Museum Special Publication No. 71, 1983.